JOURNEY OF LOVE

VOLUME II
OF
BE MY DISCIPLES

T0163318

**Not for everyone,
Only for those to whom it may concern.**

JIM REYNOLDS
1101 Witt Road
Cincinnati, OH 45255

TABLE OF CONTENTS

ACKNOWLEDGEMENT

If there is any merit to this book, it all belongs to Jeanne Guyon, because it was her book, written in the seventeenth century, <u>The Song of the Bride</u> (Republished and edited by Seed Sowers Publishing; P.O. Box 3317; Jacksonville, FL 32206; 1990); that inspired me to write this book. Without her book I would have never been able to perceive what lay behind the words found in these verses of scripture. In turn, she showed me if I truly wanted to see this <u>Song</u> as it was written by King Solomon I must see it with the eyes of my heart rather than the eyes of my mind. Thus, seeing how absolutely wonderful Guyon's book was, I questioned why I was even writing this book. Nevertheless, I continued and am glad I did, for there are those today who need to see that Guyon's book wasn't just for her day and time, some three hundred years ago; and that they are not alone in their walk with the beloved Shepherd.

May this book be a credit to <u>The Song of the Bride</u>, and in no way am I attempting to add to what Jeanne Guyon wrote. Her book was, and still is, complete in itself. I am simply writing To Whom It May Concern.

PREFACE

This book was written to be read in one sitting, two or three at the most. The objective is for the reader to gain a feel for the flow of ones' relationship to the Shepherd. Also, this book is much different from Volume I, because this time I am simply doing an exegesis of King Solomon's Song of Solomon. However, a broad exegesis is given rather than a word by word exegesis to facilitate that flow for the reader.

There are two main characters in this Song; the maiden, who represents the individual Christian; and the kinsman, who of course, is the Lord. Solomon, the author of Song, traces the development of a Christian from the point of salvation to the person's maturity as a Saint ready for the kingdom of heaven.

Italicized scripture quotes are from: Sir Lancelot C.L. Brenton's translation of the Septuagint with Apocrypha: Greek and English; published by Regency Reference Library; Zondervan Publishing House; Grand Rapids, Michigan; 1851/1986.

Also used is: Tyndale's New Testament; translated from the Greek by William Tyndale in 1534; Edited by David Daniell; published by Yale University Press, New Haven, Conn.; 1989. All other scripture quotes are from the King James Version (KJV).

INTRODUCTION

To <u>Whom It May Concern</u>: No wonder the Lord said, "Verily I say unto you, Among them that are born of women there hath not risen a greater than John the Baptist" (Matthew 11:11). John the Baptist loved Jesus more than he loved his father and mother. John loved Jesus, "...more than he loved brethren, and sisters, yea, and his own life..." (Luke 14:26). The man loved his Lord from his mother's womb to his last dying breath. He had been who he was to be. He was, "the voice of one crying in the wilderness..." (Matthew 3:3). So too are we called to be: We are to BE HIS DISCIPLES. However, the requirement of being a disciple is specific:

> *By this shall all men know that ye are my disciples, if ye have love*
> *one to another.*
> *John 13:35 KJV*

Nevertheless, being a disciple isn't going to be automatic:

> *And from the days of John the Baptist until now the kingdom of heaven*
> *suffereth violence, and the violent take it by force.*
> *Matthew 11:12 KJV*

Then there are others:

> *But whereunto shall I liken this generation? It is like unto children*
> *sitting in the markets, and calling unto their fellows, and saying, We*
> *have piped unto you, and ye have not danced; we have mourned unto*
> *you, and ye have not lamented.*
> *Matthew 11:16, 17 KJV*

What makes the difference between these two; those that "take heaven by force", and "this generation"?

Come with me on a journey, and I promise you will come to know the difference; that is if, "ye have ears to hear" (Matthew 11:15 KJV).

CHAPTER ONE

THE FIRST KISS

Let him kiss me with the kisses of his mouth: for thy love
is better than wine.

Song 1:2 (KJV)

This opening verse describes the salvation experience. It is right here a person becomes a Christian. This is the moment when a person's spirit becomes alive. When he kisses, "with the kisses of his mouth"; this is the first encounter a person has with their God. At that very instant the Lord Jesus becomes the Shepard, and we become the sheep. Our identity is now fastened to God himself.

Prior to salvation ("...kiss me with the kisses of his mouth"), we have no spirit; or we can say more accurately our spirits are dead up until salvation. People that aren't saved have no spirit (Again, more accurately, their spirits remain dead).

In the history of mankind only four people have been born saved; or are born with a live spirit. Number one was Adam: When God formed Adam of the dust of the earth, God, "...breathed into his nostrils the breath of life..." (Gen.2:7). That breath of life was spirit. Thus, Adam was created body, soul and spirit. Likewise, Eve was also created body, soul and spirit. Next, we find that John the Baptist was to be born saved (having a live spirit).

The angel said unto him:...thy wife Elizabeth shall bear thee a son,
and thou shalt call his name John. ...and he shall be filled with the
Holy Ghost, even in his mother's womb.

Luke 1:13-15 KJV

Thus, the sure sign of being saved is to be filled with the Holy Ghost (or Holy Spirit). Most preachers wrongly call this salvation experience as being "born again". The correct translation is "born from above": Check it out. The difference is serious.

To be filled with the Holy Spirit as John was; we ourselves must have a live spirit. To live in a physical world we must have a live physical body. To live in the spiritual world we must have spirits; for, "God is spirit" (John 4:24). Consequently, without a spirit it is impossible to know God; just as, without a physical body it is impossible to know anything of this planet we call earth. No body; no understanding or knowledge of the physical world. No spirit; no understanding or knowledge of God.

The fourth person born saved is the Lord and Savior, Jesus Christ.

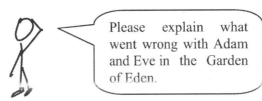

Please explain what went wrong with Adam and Eve in the Garden of Eden.

Prior to the disobedience of Adam and Eve, "…they were both naked, the man and his wife, and were not ashamed" (Gen.2:25).

Here we have these two humans with body, soul and spirit; and of the three states, the spirits were dominate. Yes, they had physical bodies, but their spirits prevailed: No doubt, due to the fact they were in constant communication with God, who as we know is spirit. Therefore, having physical bodies, they lived, however, primarily in their spirits. So much so, they didn't think of themselves as being naked: "…and were not ashamed".

However, God said that once they ate of the tree of knowledge of good and evil, "…thou shalt surely die" (Gen2:17).

Well, we know they did eat of that tree of knowledge, and we also know the two did not die. So, what happened?

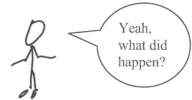

They did die. They died in their spirit.

Just look at what follows their disobedience.

> …she took of the fruit of it and ate, and gave unto her husband also with her, and he ate. And the eyes of both of them were opened, that they understood how that they were naked.
>
> Gen. 3:6, 7 Tyndale

The only way they could move so quickly from the state of spirit to such a physical state is their spirits truly died at the point of sin. Yep, the serpent was right: they would not die physically (At least not immediately; although they would now slowly begin to die physically). And God was right in that they died immediately in their spirit.

From that point forward, no one was born with a live spirit (except for John the Baptist and the Lord). From that point forward, for a man's spirit to be made alive, he would have to be kissed, "with the kisses of the Lord's mouth".

And let me tell you something. If you have to ask if you have been kissed, "with the kisses of his mouth"; that, then, is a sure sign you have not been born from above. For, to be kissed, "with the kisses of his mouth" is to know him. It is impossible to be kissed, "with the kisses of his mouth", and not know it.

Everyone that has been in love knows this. No one had to tell you that you were in love. To be in love is to know you are in love.

Do you still remember that first kiss from the one you so loved? Sure you do, because that sensation, that experience, is forever seared into your mind, body and soul. Isn't it? Neither can you ever forget that wonderful moment your spirit came alive, "with the kisses of his mouth".

Your spirit is now in union with God. You are now forever his. You have been chosen. You are as Adam first was. You are now fully body, soul and spirit.

> *And the smell of thine ointments is better than all spices: thy*
> *name is ointment poured forth;*
>
> > *Song 1:3a*

There is a new essence to your life. You begin to sense things that you never sensed before. Now that your spirit is alive your physical self seems to become even more alive. You see in ways you had never seen before. There is meaning now to each day, and most of all there is now a yearning deep inside you for that one that made you a living soul.

As when you were first in love, your every thought is towards the one you love. Now, more than then, you have a desire to seek him, the one that, "restoreth my soul" (Psalm 23:3).

> *Therefore do the young maidens love thee.*
>
> > *Song 1:3b*

You can now understand why others, which have gone before, followed after him as you now long to do.

It is not enough now to simply know him, the one that, "first loved you" (1John 4:19), and set you apart; but you seek him "as the deer panteth for water..." (Psalm 42:1). You now want him and him alone. He is your all in all. At this point you want to run after your lover.

> *They have drawn thee: we will run after thee, for the smell of thine*
> *ointments: the king has brought me into his closet: let us rejoice and*
> *be glad in thee; we will love thy breasts more than wine: righteousness*
> *loves thee.*
>
> > *Song 1:4*

You have found true happiness, and you want more. So much so, that you now seek to possess this one that first loved you, but something happens.

He leaves you!

It is here the new Christian becomes perplexed, and perhaps confused.

> *I am black, but beautiful,...look not upon me.*
>
> > *Song 1:5, 6*

Please keep in mind we must see this Song of Solomon thru the eyes of our hearts, and not by the eyes of our minds. We must at all times come to the scriptures, "in spirit..." (John

3

4:24). If we read these words from our physical senses then this becomes just another run of the mill love story.

Oh, how we must come to see what is truly happening here, because it is right here that the very essence of love exists.

OK, let's quickly recap, and this time we will follow what happens with respect to the maiden in this song (She represents us as individual Christians), and her quest to be with her kinsman, sometimes referred to as the shepherd or beloved (Who represents the Lord as described by Solomon).

A) The most extraordinary event in life has just happened to the maiden.
B) Nothing in the physical world can compare.

C) Her normal senses became alive as never before.

D) She comes to understand what it was that others (Christians) had known for so long, and why others sought the kinsman.
E) She runs after this one that has touched her so.
F) In that pursuit there is nothing but joy.

G) And there is a sense of security.

H) And it is only meet and right to seek the Lord.
I) But the beloved disappears.

J) The maiden now has time to reflect, and finds within parts of herself that she dislikes.

K) Nevertheless, she knows she has truly been loved of God.

A) The shepherd, "kissed me with the kisses of his mouth" (1:2)
B) "…for thy breasts (love) are better than wine" (1:2).
C) "and the smell of thine ointments is better than all spices: thy name is ointment poured forth" (1:3)
D) "…therefore do the young maidens love thee. They have drawn thee" (1:3, 4).

E) "…we will run after thee,…" (1:4).

F) "…for the smell of thine ointments:…let us rejoice and be glad in thee; we will love thy breasts more than wine (1:4).
G) "…the king has brought me into his closet:' (1:4).
H) "…righteousness loves thee" (1:4).

I) We know this has happened because of the maidens' reaction in verses five and six, and by what follows in verse seven.
J) "I am black, but beautiful …look not upon me, because I am dark, because the sun has looked unfavorably upon me…" (1:5, 6).
K) "…as the tents of Keder, as the curtains of Solomon… Tell me, thou whom my soul loves" (1:5; 1:7).

Much has happened to the maiden in a very short period of time, and a most curious part of all these changes is that no sooner has she become alive in her spirit than the very one responsible for all these wonderful happenings takes off and disappears.

This seems so cruel and insensitive on the part of her beloved shepherd: but it is not so; really it's not.

Then please explain.

God's world is different from man's world. For years the maiden had lived totally in man's world. Now that she has a spirit within her, she can begin to live more and more in God's world of the spirit. However, for the maiden, there is much to be learned, and it is the beloved shepherd that becomes the teacher, and the very first thing the maiden is to learn is that there are absolutes in God's world. This is so very unlike man's world where everything is relative (or so men think). Consequently, the maiden must change to fit into this new world of the spirit, but oh, how we try so hard to change God instead.

At the very center of this change is the nature of love. The maiden's first lesson is her most important lesson: She is to learn that there are two kinds of love: man's love, and God's love.

The maiden's first reaction to her salvation experience was to possess the one that gave her this experience. This is the way men love.

You see, man's love is a possessive love, and in reality, this is not love at all. Possessive love is pride. In fact, possessive love is your very basic form of pride. Man's love is pride wrapped with ribbons of goodness and many feely-goods.

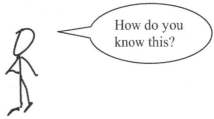

How do you know this?

Easy: just look at the results of man's love, or more accurately put, possessive love. When a person can no longer control or possess the one they "love"; this so called love turns to anger. Sure, look around at our marriages. When the couple first gets married; oh, are they so much in "love". Things are so wonderful. They truly have strong feelings one to the other. Then years later these two wonderful people become worst enemies. Not only do they get a divorce, but they out and out hate each other. What went wrong?

Nothing went wrong. It was all wrong from the start, because the love each had for the other wasn't love; not really. They each loved each other as long as there was a sense of control or possession involved. Once one of the two lost control of the other then these other feelings of anger and hate surface. Nevertheless, the anger and hate were always there from the beginning because what they called love was in reality pride. For it is pride that seeks to possess and control; not love, at least not God's love.

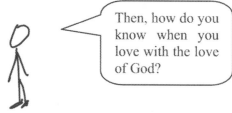

You have to take love to its conclusion. Then and only then do you know if you love with God's love or man's love.

There is no end to God's love. If you love with God's love you will love your enemies (Matthew 5:44): whereas, man's love ends when we can no longer possess the object of our affections. With God's love it doesn't matter what the other does to you. You will always love them no matter what they do to you. You will even love those that hate you.

On the other hand, man's love is pride, and we know this by looking at the end results of that love. True love would never have bitterness, hate, anger and even death at its conclusion. Only pride contains those results.

Now, the highest form of pride is to seek to possess God. It is one thing to possess another human being, but pride of all pride is to seek to control God, and this is exactly what the maiden was trying to do when she, "…ran after thee" (Song 1:4).

She wasn't aware this is what she was doing, nor could anyone tell her that running after the shepherd was not love at all, but was an act of pride. Nor, can we tell that young couple at the marriage alter that what they call love for each other is nothing but the pride of control. Nor, can we tell so many of those well meaning church goers that their prayers are not love for God, but their prayers are nothing but prideful attempts to control and manipulate God.

Oh, dear reader do we love God with man's love, or are we loving God with his love?

This right here is what the <u>Song of Solomon</u> is all about. The rest of this book details how the beloved shepherd develops in the maiden the very love of God.

All Christians, like the maiden, must learn God's love. We do not just naturally love with the love of God. The love of God must be developed in us step by step.

Non-Christians don't even have the capacity to love with God's love. It is impossible for an unsaved person to love: to truly love as God loves. Not until the moment he kisses "with the kisses of his mouth" do we even have the capacity to truly love. Also, it is only the shepherd which can bring us into this love of God.

Just as the maiden has to learn God's love, so too must all Christians have to learn this love. So, come with me as we follow the maiden in her journey of love.

CHAPTER TWO

THE WAY OF THE SHEPHERDS

I am black, but beautiful, ye daughters of Jerusalem, as the tents
of Kedar, as the curtains of Solomon. Look not upon me, because
I am dark, because the sun has looked unfavorably upon me:
                                            Song 1:5, 6

As we discussed earlier, the first reaction after being filled with the spirit of God is to reach for the "author...of our faith" (Heb. 12:2). When he leaves, then we immediately look within ourselves and ponder at how corrupt and depraved we actually are. Oh sure, we are now a child of God, but how could he love one such as I? Not until we see him as he is, can we truly see ourselves as we are. This is what is happening here with the maiden. God's holiness is contrasted with her depravity.

Isn't it wonderful that, "while we were yet sinners, Christ died for us" (Rom. 5:8). In other words, we don't have to be a good person before we are saved. God takes us just as we are when he kisses us "with the kisses of his mouth" (Song 1:2).

...my mother's sons strove with me; they made me keeper in
the vineyards; I have not kept my own vineyard.
                                            Song 1:6

The initial reaction from those around us is often negative (not always, but more often than not). The maiden's immediate family noticed a change had taken place within her, and they reacted by giving her extra chores. However, they have no idea what the change is. They simply know that she had changed.

In a way any change is threatening to most folks; especially a change with no explanation. Perhaps the maiden herself can't explain exactly what happened. She too, simply knows she has changed. Oh, a good change; that is not at question, but change is a change, is a change. So, at this point the maiden feels a little guilty she has received something so wonderful and the rest of her family hasn't. Therefore, the maiden tends her family's vineyard even to the neglect of her own. In other words, the maiden's prayer life suffers at the expense of the families other needs. The maiden also neglects her Bible study time, and she might even curtail her church going in an effort to please or pacify her immediate family.

This is a typical reaction; especially when the other family members are not saved. Also, the maiden is new at all this Christian stuff. So, she simply operates out of a natural reflex action. However, this should be a temporary state, and the maiden must come out of this attitude as quickly as possible.

This is exactly what she does. In fact, the maiden does the very best thing. She talks to her beloved shepherd in prayer, and asks him what to do next:

Tell me thou whom my soul loves, where thou tendest thy flock,
where thou causest them to rest at noon, lest I become as one
that is veiled by the flocks of thy companions.

Song 1:7

We must understand when the shepherd leaves her it is never for good. In fact, as we will find out later, he never really leaves her; not really. It is his presence that leaves her, and in one sense she truly feels alone; but deep down, if she hasn't already sensed it, she will find out that she is never, never abandoned by her shepherd. She will also later learn that there is purpose in the shepherd's leaving her.

Tell me, thou whom my soul loves.

Song 1:7

This is so wonderful. Already the maiden knows deep within her soul that she is alive with love. She is already sure of her salvation. She knows, no matter what happens her soul and her savior are one. Nevertheless, she is still searching for him.

In and of itself, there is nothing wrong with her desire to be with him, but as we shall see, it is imperative the shepherd continues to come and go. We must also trust him. He knows what is best for each of us, and we will also come to see it is normal for every Christian to experience this coming and going of the Lord and beloved shepherd.

He answers her:

If thou know not thyself, thou fair one among women, go thou
forth by the footsteps of the flocks, and feed thy kids by the
shepherds tents.

Song 1:8

The way of the Lord is the way of the shepherds. In other words, the Christian walk is the same walk as everybody else. We Christians are not going to be treated any differently from anybody else. Believers must travel the same path as unbelievers. In this life, Christians get no special deals: "...for he maketh his sun to rise on the evil and on the good, and sendeth rain on the just and on the unjust" (Matt. 5:45).

If the cars of unbelievers get flat tires, then Christians get flat tires too. The just have to pay their light bills the same as the unjust. Christians lock their car keys in the car the same as everybody else. Our children get sick the same as all children. There are no extra privileges for king's kids. The Lord paid taxes the same as everybody else (Matt. 17:27).

There is very good reason that believers must go the way of the shepherd. Just think about it: If Christians received special treatment then the lost would seek God for what they too could get from God, and that would negate the need for faith. Most of all, however, if we received special privileges there would be no room for love.

The beloved shepherd follows his answer to the maiden with a true expression of love:

I have likened thee, my companion, to my horses in the chariots
of Pharao. How are thy cheeks beautiful as those of a dove, thy
neck as chains.

Song 1:9, 10

He didn't put the maiden down for asking a question. No, no a thousand times no. She is truly seeking him, and even though he can't allow himself to be possessed by her; he still longs for her. Oh, how he loves her, and he tells her so.

As the relationship develops between the maiden and the shepherd, we will discover that the shepherd becomes more and more intimate with the maiden. If he could, the shepherd would want nothing better than to sweep the maiden away with him now, but he knows only too well the maiden simply isn't ready for the full effects of God's love. It would be too much too soon.

It takes time to shift from seeing with the eyes of our head to the eyes of our heart, and to learn to love with God's love rather than to love as men do. However, there is no way to convince the maiden she isn't ready for true love yet; not really. Therefore, the shepherd has to come and go, and come and go: each time drawing the maiden ever so gently to the place where she will finally be able to truly love with the love of God.

> *So long as the king was at table, my spikenard gave forth its smell.*
> *My kinsman is to me a bundle of myrrh; he shall lie between my*
> *breasts. My kinsman is to me a cluster of camphor in the vineyards*
> *of Engaddi.*
>
> *Song 1:12-14*

Here the maiden, as she travels the way of the shepherds, contemplates what her new lover means to her. Here at the beginning of her journey, the maiden sees the shepherd (kinsman) in ways she can still possess him. She continues to want to hold him, possess him still: and in a roundabout way she is still seeking to manipulate the shepherd into her arms.

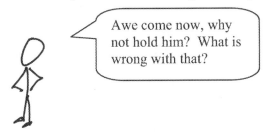

At first glance her wanting to hold her beloved seems so innocent and sweet, but there are in fact serious repercussions if the shepherd allows her to have her way. Right now the kinsman seems unduly harsh and insensitive, but please be patient with the shepherd. He truly knows what he is doing. He cannot let the maiden trick him, no matter how sweet and innocent she may be; and throughout this journey the shepherd remains gentle with the maiden; and never does he scold her either. He simply responds to each and every prayer of hers:

> *Behold thou art fair, my companion; behold, thou art fair; thine*
> *eyes are doves.*
>
> *Song 1:15*

She responds:

> *Behold, thou art fair, my kinsman, yea, beautiful, overshadowing*
> *our bed. The beams of our house are cedars, our ceilings are of*
> *cypress.*
>
> *Song 1:16-2:1*

Notice the maiden now calls the shepherd her kinsman. Nevertheless, she continues to seek to control him, and make him hers. Yet, he continues to respond gently, yet firmly keeping his distance.

As a lily among thorns, so is my companion among the daughters.
Song 2:2

Can we not begin to see the value in the shepherd not letting the maiden gain control and possess him? If he allowed her to hold him, he then would, in fact, be contributing to her sense of pride; and in a real sense he would be an accomplice to her eventual downfall; because he would be helping her strengthen her flesh; and that is the last thing she needs. No, he must stay away from her. Oh, how he must stay away. Therefore, he continues to come and go.

Please don't misunderstand. The shepherd truly longs for the maiden (And we will see this more and more as we go); but he being the initiator of this love affair has a responsibility to keep her and bring her: "that she should be holy and without blemish" (Eph. 5:27).

CHAPTER THREE

SET LOVE BEFORE ME

*As the apple among the trees of the wood, so is my kinsman among
the sons, I desire his shadow, and sat down, and his fruit was sweet
in my throat. Bring me into the wine house; set love before me.
Strengthen me with perfumes, stay me with apples: for I am wounded
with love.*

Song 2:3-5

The maiden is reflecting back upon her new state of being. A whole new world has been spread out before her. Not only is all this spirit world new, but it is all hers. She is fast realizing she is being called to be an active participant in this new world. Yet, more than that; she has also comprehended she is an heir to this spiritual realm.

For ye are all the sons of God, by the faith which is in Christ Jesus…
If ye be Christ's then are ye…heirs by promise…If thou be the son,
thou art also the heir of God through Christ.

Gal.3:26, 29, 4:7 Tyndale

In one sense, she is delighted beyond understanding; and in another way, she is overwhelmed by it all. Most of all; however, for the first time in her life she has experienced honest and true love. This is a love that goes to the very core of her soul, and is so pure; and such a sure love that the only way to describe it is for her to say, "I am wounded with love".

*His left hand shall be under my head, and his right hand shall
embrace me. I have charged you, ye daughters of Jerusalem, by
the powers and by the virtues of the field, that ye do not rouse
or wake my love, until he please.*

Song 2:6, 7

These words are spoken three times in this book. The kinsman (or shepherd) is making a pronouncement. He announces to all concerned that he is indeed in complete control of the maiden's life and soul.

You see, the maiden at this very moment still does not sense the kinsman's presence. She still seeks him. Yet, without her knowledge he is holding her in his arms at that very moment. Not only is he in complete control, he is also announcing to the entire spiritual realm that they are to keep hands off. This maiden belongs to him, and no one is to interfere with this relationship. He is jealous over her.

Yes, our God is a jealous God (Ex. 20:5 & others), and let it be known he is in complete control. He holds each and every one of us in his arms. We may not sense his presence. We may be looking for him in the far distant horizon, but all along, he has hold of each one of us, for God is indeed a jealous God.

The voice of my kinsman! Behold, he comes leaping over the
mountains, bounding over the hills.

Song 2:8

He never fails. Just when the maiden needed assurance; up bounds her kinsman.

At this point in their relationship, the maiden sees her Lord as a deer bounding over and around the rocks on the mountain tops. Deer are so graceful, and at the same time they are so sure footed even on those craggy mountain slops. While others creep with fear and trembling as they make their way over and around those steep and dangerous mountains; the deer leap, and even play as they bound swiftly in and out of those same crevices. Yes, the Lord is as "hind's feet on high places" (Habakkuk 3:19).

The kinsman is like a deer in another respect.

Like a deer, he is allusive, and nearly impossible to hold. Also, like a deer, the maiden must let the kinsman come to her when he is ready, and if she gets too close to him, he flees as a deer flees. Likewise, the kinsman is as quiet as a deer: Without notice or even the slightest movement he may watch the maiden by the hour completely unnoticed.

When we lived in a log cabin nestled beneath the shadows of the Blue Ridge Mountains of North Carolina, I would often take off by myself, and hike far up onto the top of those mountains: no provisions, no trails, and no one else, and I would spend the afternoon alone in the meadows at the top. Water would bubble forth from a rock. I would drink that clean cold water then would lie down on some grass and doze off.

More often than not; after a few minutes, I would sense the presence of someone watching me. I would argue with myself, "There is no one up here besides me". Nevertheless, I could still sense a pair of eyes on me. Slowly I would turn my head; first one way, then the other: nothing. A few minutes later, I would again look around, and suddenly our eyes met. A deer was lying in a thicket only a few yards from me. He had been there from the beginning. I hadn't been alone after all; and no sooner had I spotted the deer; than he stood up and silently disappeared; and was gone.

So often the Lord is like that. If we aren't careful, we will spook him, and he will be gone.

Why? Why is he like that?

He leaves for the same reason the deer left me. You see, that deer knew what I was thinking the very moment I spotted him. He knew my desire was to go over and hold him, and how true that was, because that is exactly what went through my mind when our eyes met. He was so beautiful, so majestic, that my desire was to move slowly towards him so I could touch him; hold him; and yes, possess him.

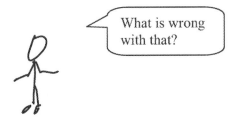

That is pride. Who am I to think I can possess a deer. That would ruin everything. Can't we see that the moment I took possess of him he would no longer be who he is: a majestic free spirited creature of the wild. Likewise, the Lord cannot let us possess him, for the moment we were to take hold of him he ceases to be who he is: God. Besides, who am I to think I can possess God. That is pride. No, that is the height of pride. Therefore, the Lord must be as a deer to come and go at will, and the most we can do is to appreciate the moments we do get a glimpse of him, however fleeting those moments may be. The maiden has finally learned to look for her kinsman as one would anticipate the comings and goings of a deer.

> *My kinsman is like a roe or a young heart on the mountains of*
> *Bethel: behold, he is behind our wall, looking through the*
> *windows, peering through the lattices.*
> *Song 2:9*

She has learned well to simply "be", and not to seek to possess the kinsman when he comes around. She lets him come and go at his pleasure, and she is thankful for the few glimpses she gets of him every now and then. Now, she is ready for her next step in her journey of love. He now calls her to come.

> *My kinsman answers, and says to me, rise up, come, my companion*
> *fair one, my dove. For, behold, the winter is past, the rain is gone,*
> *it has departed. The flowers are seen in the land; the time of pruning*
> *has arrived; the voice of the turtledove has been heard in our land.*
> *the fig-tree has put forth its young figs, the vines put forth tender*
> *grape, they yield a smell: arise, come, my companion, my fair one,*
> *my dove; yea, come.*
> *Song 2:10-13*

Where is he taking her?

To the maiden it doesn't matter where her kinsman is taking her. All she cares about is that he called her. However, one thing we do know from this calling is that he is calling her to a task (or ministry) of some kind. The kinsman wants the maiden to enter into a work; and this work has been an on going work in which the kinsman is so very familiar.

The maiden can tell that this work has something to do with fruit bearing, "…the time of pruning has arrived…the fig-tree has put forth its young figs, the vine put forth the tender grape…"

What a wonderful ministry she is called to. She is called to help him bring forth fruit of many kinds and sights, sounds, and smells all around are lovely and sweet, "…the flowers are seen…the voice of the turtle-dove has been heard…the figs…and grapes…yield a smell".

The maiden couldn't be any happier for two reasons. First, she is finally called by her lover to join with him in a wonderful ministry. Secondly, and perhaps most of all, she finally knows where her lover stays.

My kinsman is mine, and I am his: he feeds his flock among the lilies.
Song 2:16

She has the assurance of her salvation. He has confided in her, and he has called her to come out of herself to work with him.

There is no question the kinsman would have called the maiden earlier, but he couldn't afford to do so, because she still wanted to hold on to him. She had to get to the place where she was able to simply let things be as they are, and not try to control, or manipulate the kinsman. The moment she could let things be, then, and only then, was she ready to enter into a ministry. However, something happened at this juncture.

Take us the little foxes that spoil the vines: for our vines put forth
tender grapes.
Song 2:15

Little foxes represent the devil and his demons. Up until this time the devil didn't need to get actively involved in the maiden's life: for, as long as she sought control of the relationship, she was doing more damage than he could do. However, now that the maiden was in submission to her kinsman her own vines are finally putting forth fruit (Compare this verse with 1:6: where she didn't care for her own vineyard).

As long as her vineyard wasn't producing fruit; then why should the devil and his demons bother her? Of course not, the demons aren't stupid; as long as things are going sour thru neglect, why bother. But the moment our lives begin to produce fruit; then, as quick as a fox the demons will invade and seek to, "spoil those vines".

Until the day dawn, and the shadows depart, turn, my kinsman, be
thou like to a roe or young heart on the mountains of ravines.
Song 2:17

Oh, how the maiden has matured in her new life of salvation and the spirit. Not only does she no longer seek to possess her lover, but she is now so confident in her relationship that she is satisfied the way things are.

It is right here, between 2:17 and 3:1 that so many Christians ere. Just as the maiden thinks she has arrived (after all, she has a full-time ministry), they too think they have arrived when they enter a ministry or pastorate. Yet, the truth of the matter is she and these others have barely begun their journey. Thus, it is tempting to stay right here.

CHAPTER FOUR

HIM WHOM MY SOUL LOVES

*By night on my bed I sought him whom my soul loves: I sought
him, but found him not; I called him, but he hearkened not to me.*
Song 3:1

No sooner had the maiden found where her kinsman feeds his flock; he vanishes. She thought she knew him. What went wrong? After all, she had finally learned not to try to control him, and her life was now bearing fruit. However, what the maiden is learning is that the Lord knows her better than she knows herself. Although she no longer sought to control her beloved; the reality of the situation is she had learned an even better way to control him than before.

True, overtly she no longer sought to possess the kinsman; however, in an inwardly or subversive way she was still seeking to control him.

I don't get it. This doesn't make sense.

Oh, how depraved we are. Yet, there is no way for us to see the depths of our depravity until we truly get involved in seeking God with, "all our heart, and with all our soul, and with all our mind" (Matthew 22:37). Then and only then, can we even begin to see ourselves as we truly are, and only God can wash us clean of this condition (See Romans chapter seven and chapter four of Vol. I).

The maiden doesn't believe she has a problem. In fact, she is convinced that her kinsman is the one with the problem. He left her. She didn't leave him, and how could he leave at the very moment her, "vines put forth tender grapes"? Something has to be wrong with him; not her. After all, she loves him so, "...I sought him whom my soul loves".

Oh, come now, aren't you stretching things?

Look at what she does next.

*I will rise now, and go about in the city, in the market-places, and
in the streets, and I will seek him whom my soul loves: I sought him,
but found him not.*
Song 3:2

Is that control, or is that control?

Sure it's control. She doesn't get what she wants; so, she goes out to get it anyway.

Not until the kinsman leaves her again is she able to see once again that she still has the urge to hold on to him. Oh, how strong our flesh is; and it, the flesh, continues to be this way long into our walk with the Lord. Paul's letter to the Galatian church speaks of this condition: "…the flesh lusteth contrary to the spirit, and the spirit contrary to the flesh. These are contrary one to the other, so that ye cannot do that which ye would" (Galatians 5:17 Tyndale).

It is right here some cease to walk any further with the Lord. They have been called to a ministry, and that is good enough for them. To these the ministry becomes greater than the Lord himself. However, the maiden didn't stop. She continued to seek her beloved.

> *The watchman who go their rounds in the city found me. I said, have*
> *ye seen him whom my soul loves.*
>
> *Song 3:3*

The watchmen are pastors, ministers, clergy etc., and notice they didn't know where to find the kinsman. Don't misunderstand, pastors and such are important in the overall scheme of things, but we must come to see that this spiritual journey of love is an individual journey, and not even the clergy can help us. Even if they did know where to find the kinsman, they still can't help; not really.

> *It was as a little while after I parted from them, that I found him whom*
> *my soul loves: I held him, and did not let him go, until I brought him*
> *into my mother's house, and into the chamber of her that conceived me.*
>
> *Song 3:4*

This verse is the maiden's dream or wishful thinking of what she would like to do: not that it was done. She had been greatly disappointed in not being able to find her kinsman. Also, everyone including her pastor (watchmen) now know she has lost her Lord; and not only has she lost her Lord, but we know from verse 3:1 she had great plans all figured out for the two of them.

A lot has happened to the maiden since her salvation experience. She has grown a great deal in a short time. She has come to know for the first time true love: A love that reaches to her very soul, "…him whom my soul loves". She has indeed found one of the places where her kinsman spends his time, "…he feeds his flocks among the lilies". He is hers and she is his. She knows that for sure now. She has a real ministry, and this is but the beginning of greater things to come. Yet, at the very point she is basking in all these new found feelings and experience; along with the fact she can finally begin to contemplate what the future holds for her; then, just like that, he is gone, and this time he has truly disappeared. Even the watchmen don't know where her beloved has gone. Most of all, however, all her acquaintances can see she isn't all that she is cracked up to be. So, the maiden sulks or even gets depressed; and it is here, at the point of depression, that she day-dreams of what things could or should really be like. She dreams of holding her kinsman. She even dreams of total and complete oneness with him.

> *I have charged you, O daughters of Jerusalem, by the powers and by the*
> *virtues of the field, that ye rouse not nor awake my love, until he please.*
>
> *Song 3:5*

At her lowest point, the Lord announces to the spiritual realm that he indeed holds her securely as she can be held. The maiden is unaware of verse 3:5. She cannot sense the kinsman holding her. This holding is being done completely in the spiritual realm; and the maiden, at this point, cannot comprehend the spiritual realm all that well yet.

We can now begin to see that our darkest moments are in fact our most blessed moments. For, the times we feel most alienated from the Lord, are in reality, the times we are the closest to him.

Oh, how we must come to cherish our dark times. We must come to praise God for all things; and it is here so many of us miss the true essence of the Christian walk.

When problems enter our lives, the first thing we seek to do is to eliminate those problems. We don't like pain, so we take immediate steps to relieve ourselves of this pain: even to the point of anger towards anyone which suggests otherwise.

Our prayers become urgent pleas for God to take away the pain or problem: When all along, it is God himself who brought these problems upon us so we could grow from the pain.

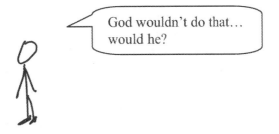

Notice what happens next.

> *Who is this that comes up from the wilderness as pillars of smoke, perfumed with myrrh and frankincense, with all powders of the perfumer? Behold Solomon's bed; sixty mighty men of the mighty ones of Israel are about it. They all hold a sword, being expert in war: every man has his sword upon his thigh because of fear by night.*
>
> *Song 3:6-8*

God doesn't leave us to ourselves during these times of trial. If he brings pain upon us he also brings with it a way out (1 Corinthians 10:13). The problem with so many of us is we don't like God's solutions. Actually, we don't like his problems either; nevertheless, this is the way God operates. In fact, this right here is the beauty of the Song of Solomon. For, it is here God reveals to us his way of love. First Corinthians, chapter thirteen, gives us a definition of love. This song here explains that love in action.

Here comes the maiden's rescue. It comes in the form of a pillar of cloud. This pillar of smoke can be seen from far off. It must be powerful indeed. Oh, thank you Lord, for at her greatest time of need you send such a marvelous and powerful remedy: or so it seems.

Powerful, yes; remedy, yes; marvelous, that remains to be seen. Let's take a look at this rescue team.

First, the pillar of smoke comes from the wilderness, and as we know from other studies; the wilderness is a place of testing. It is a place in which the flesh is dealt with. Thus, we can conclude that the maiden will need her flesh to be subdued.

Secondly, the pillars of smoke smell wonderful. However, as wonderful as they smell, the ingredients are myrrh and frankincense which symbolize sorrow and suffering.

Yes God's way out for the maiden is with sorrow and suffering.

Sorry, but this right here is the "way of escape" Paul talks about in First Corinthians 10:13. We are never to get away from this fact right here. To learn the love of God, we must suffer. Not maybe suffer; or suffer now and then; but we must actually embrace sorrow and suffering as a way of life.

It is tempting to stop right here in one's journey of love: For some, it is hard to accept such sorrow and suffering into one's life. It would be so easy to find a church where the pains and problems won't follow. However, the maiden pressed on, and so must we.

There is a third part to the way of escape. The Lord gives us his word, the Bible. This is what the "sixty mighty men" are all about. Each one carries a sword, which we know represents God's word as found in the Bible. Therefore, when sorrow and suffering enter your life, embrace them along with the scriptures; and something profound will begin to take place in your prayer life. Slowly but surely, you will begin to pray the scriptures. Verse and prayer will become one. As you immerse yourself in the scriptures, prayer will flow from deep within your spirit until those prayers rise to heaven before the very throne of God, "as pillars of smoke, perfumed with myrrh and frankincense".

King Solomon made himself a litter of woods of Lebanon. He made the pillars of it silver, the bottom of it gold, the covering of it scarlet, in the midst of it a pavement of love, for the daughters of Jerusalem. Go forth, ye daughters of Sion, and behold King Solomon, with the crown wherewith his mother crowned him, in the day of his espousals, and in the day of the gladness of his heart.

Song 3:9-11

These verses reflect a transition is about to take place. The maiden is about to move into a whole new realm; for this is what is in store for those that truly do embrace altogether everything God brings into their lives.

The maiden is about to move from her calling into her election (Being chosen: Matthew 20:16; 22:14; 24:22; Mark 13:20; 13:27; 2Peter 1:10; and others). In the present these two are separate and distinct. In the end, calling and election are as one.

God continually places before us this journey of love. He doesn't hide a thing. After all, this is what the Gospel is all about. He is telling us from the get go the path to joy and peace can only be obtained by embracing suffering and sorrow. However, these, "many called" are as the woman in Luke 11:27 who also misses the essence of the Gospel, when she said to Jesus as he was on the way to the cross, "Blessed is the womb that bare thee, and the paps which thou hast sucked". The Lord quickly rebuked her, "But he said, Yea rather, blessed are they that hear the word of God, and keep it" (Luke 11:28).

The woman missed the whole meaning of the Lord's presence. She could only see the goodness of it all. She had no concept of what the Gospel is all about. That is why the Lord said what he did. For, the essence of the Gospel can only be experienced through obedience to that very same Gospel. Yes, knowing it can only be found in the keeping of it.

Oh, how thankful am I that the maiden chose to go on, and may you also continue. For, we are about to find out moving from chapter three of this song to chapter four is as dramatic as moving from unbelief to becoming a believer. However, the transition this time is much slower and more deliberate. Being born from above came in as a flash of lightening; election comes as the dawning of the sun.

Verses 3:9-11 speak of the day Solomon was crowned king of Israel. Now, when Solomon was born, he was at that very moment heir to the thrown of David. Nevertheless, Solomon had some growing up to do before he actually obtained the actual power of the throne. Likewise, the maiden was called from the moment she was kissed, "with the kisses of his mouth"; and she too, like Solomon, had much growing up to do before she could actually experience her election.

Also, from the time Solomon was born until the day he assumed the throne, he could have chosen not to be king. Likewise, the maiden, from the moment she was saved until now; she too could have called it quits. However, Solomon continued, and so did the maiden.

CHAPTER FIVE

NO SPOT IN THEE

*Behold, thou art fair, my companion; behold, thou art fair; thine
eyes are doves, beside thy veil: thy hair is as flocks of goats, that
have appeared from Galaad. Thy teeth are as flocks of shorn sheep,
that have gone up from the washing; all of them bearing twins, and
there is not a barren one among them. Thy lips are as a thread of
scarlet, and thy speech is comely: like the rind of a pomegranate is
thy cheek without thy veil. Thy neck is as the tower of David, that
built for an armoury: a thousand shields hang upon it, and all darts
of mighty men. Thy two breasts are as two twin fawns, that feed
among the lilies.*

Song 4:1-5

Between chapter three and here in four, the maiden has spent perhaps years with her pillars of
myrrh (suffering) and frankincense (sorrow). She has also immersed herself in the word of God
during this period, and the "sixty mighty men of the mighty ones of Israel" are constantly present
with her to protect her from the assaults of the enemy.

The maiden makes the transition from called to chosen, and she is immediately met by
her kinsman who has been waiting patiently, yet anxiously for her.

Oh, how beautiful she looks to her kinsman. The maiden has matured so much during the
dark part of her journey, for these verses are full of descriptions of being fruitful and mature
(Again, please understand, we must look at her with the eyes of our heart; not with the eyes of
our head. More than ever, we are to use our spirit for understanding, not our minds):

"hair as flocks of goats"	= fullness
"teeth as flocks of shorn sheep…and there is not a barren one among them"	= completeness
"thy speech is comely: like the rind of pomegranate"	= completely satisfactory
"neck is as the tower of David,…"	= strong and stable
"thy two breasts are as twin fawns…"	= mature and able to nurture

Not until now is the maiden ready to nourish others (truly nourish others). Prior to this
time, the maiden had a ministry, and it was there she could help others, and minister to the needs
of others, but now; she is finally able to bring spiritual nourishment to others. Yes, before the
maiden knew of the spiritual realm, but now she herself is part of that spiritual realm. However,
before she can be actively involved in that realm, one more step has to be made. She has yet to
go to the mountain of myrrh, and to the hill of frankincense. In other words, she is to go to the
cross on Calvary.

*Until the day dawn, and the shadows depart, I will betake me to
the mountain of myrrh, and to the hill of frankincense.*

Song 4:6

From the very moment the maiden was kissed "with the kisses of his mouth", the shepherd has been slowly but firmly bringing her to the cross on Calvary.

Can we now see more clearly why he couldn't let her possess him? He had a plan for her, and that plan was the cross. The shepherd had to come and go as a deer or roe, for the maiden would follow in no other way. Also, each attempt to possess the shepherd was in fact an attempt to keep the shepherd from taking her to the cross. In a way, she sensed all along the cross lay before her. In fact, the cross is the destination for every Christian: no cross; no Christ.

Everything up until now has been in preparation for the cross. However, our cross isn't something we set out to find. As we follow the beloved Lord, the cross will find us; and when that time comes we will know it.

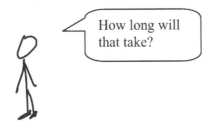

How long will that take?

A good friend of mine often asked a similar question. He would say, "If I knew where my cross was I would go get it right now".

I couldn't tell him; for, it isn't up to any of us to know where someone's cross is. When the time is right, the Lord will lead you there. Our responsibility is to be ready; and to be ready, we are to be as clay in the potter's hand. Simply let the Lord have his way with us through obedience to his every desire.

My friend did become clay in the potter's hand, and about two years later I had the privilege of conducting the marriage ceremony for him and his lovely bride.

The wedding began. The bride came down the isle arm and arm with her father. Her father placed her hand into the groom's hand, and the two came forward standing about three feet in front of me. We had to wait for the special music to stop before I could continue with the service. While I was facing the two of them, just waiting; I noticed my friend was looking above my head at something. Then in a hushed but serious expression he, now looking at me, said, "Jim, I found my cross".

I didn't know exactly what he was talking about, and unable to move without distracting from the special music that was still playing, my friend motioned with his eyes to a huge cross that was on the wall behind me. Then his eyes cut over to his lovely bride standing at his side (By the way, his bride was oblivious to what we were discussing). "My cross, I've found my cross".

Yes, marriage was indeed his cross (Not only his, but their cross together). The first five years of their marriage were the worst five years of their lives. Nevertheless, they stuck it out, and as badly as it felt, those two embraced suffering and sorrow until there will be therefore, "no spot in thee".

However, your cross doesn't have to come out of something bad in your life. The cross for some comes from something good. There was another young couple I married, and their marriage was perfect from the very first day they met. They where both strong and very mature in the Lord. Their marriage was truly a marriage made in heaven. Then about four years into the marriage, the wife contracted a very debilitating disease, and for the next six years she became a spiritual pillar of strength for all those around her. The feebler her physical body became, the stronger was her spiritual stature. The weaker she became, the stronger was their love for each other. Then she died. The husband was devastated, yet he continued in the way. Yes, marriage was his cross as well, and just like the other couple, there was found, "no spot in thee".

> *Thou art all fair, my companion, and there is no spot in thee.*
> *Song 4:7*

Not until we have born our cross is there "no spot in thee". Now, and only now, can the maiden truly be in unity with her kinsman. Until the cross does its work in us can we be who we were meant to be. Oh, there is more to come, much more, but the maiden was now in unity with her Lord. From that first kiss she was destined to be his bride, now she is that bride, for there is "no spot in thee".

> *Come from Libanus, my bride, come from Libanus: thou shalt come*
> *and pass from the top of faith, from the top of Sanir and Hermon,*
> *from the lions' dens, from the mountains of the leopards.*
> *Song 4:8*

The relationship has matured. There is now a unity between the maiden and her kinsman that was not possible prior to the maiden having gone "to the mountain of myrrh and to the hill of frankincense". The bond between the two has strengthened; a bond that can only grow more and more in oneness, one with the other. It is here no words need to be spoken between these two, but just the opposite takes place. The kinsman can scarcely hold his tongue. He bubbles over with affection for his maiden. The kinsman had wonderful words for his maiden prior to the cross, but he now gushes forth. He cannot say enough about her from this point on.

Did he love her before?

Sure he did, but prior to the cross we can't receive what he has to say to us. Prior to the cross we are still caught up with ourselves. We are still too full of pride. However, "if we be dead with Christ, we believe that we shall also live with him (Romans 6:8). Death brings life. For the first time in her life she finally is truly alive. Before she heard words, now she hears her beloved's voice. It takes a person of sorrow to know another of sorrow. Only those that suffer can understand another who suffers. Now, he has something to say to her, for only now, "doeth she hath ears to hear".

> *My sister, my spouse, thou hast ravished my heart; thou hast*
> *ravished my heart with one of thine eyes, with one chain of thy*
> *neck. How beautiful are thy breasts, my sister, my spouse!*
> *How much more beautiful are thy breast than wine, and the*
> *smell of thy garments than all spices: thy lips drop honeycomb,*
> *my spouse: honey and milk are under thy tongue: and the smell*
> *of thy garments is as the smell of Libanus. My sister, my spouse*
> *is a garden enclosed; a garden enclosed, a fountain sealed. Thy*
> *shoots are a garden of pomegranates, with the fruit of choice*
> *berries; camphor, with spikenard: spikenard and saffron, calamus*
> *and cinnamon; with all woods of Libanus, myrrh, aloes, with all*
> *chief spices: a fountain of a garden, and a well of water springing*

and gurgling from Libanus.

Song 4:9-15

We are reminded again that we are to look with the eyes of our hearts, our spirits; not in a physical sense, or with the eyes of our head. When the beloved kinsman looks at the maiden he is looking from his spirit. In no way is he thinking in fleshly terms.

What a difference this description is from those found in Song 1:9-11 and Song 4:1-5. Moments prior to the cross the maiden is breath-taking to her kinsman: only hours later the maiden is now full and complete. The cross has done its work.

CHAPTER SIX

WOUNDED WITH LOVE

Awake, O north wind; and come, O south; and blow through my garden, and let my spices flow out. Let my kinsman come down into his garden, and eat the fruit of his choice berries. I am come into my garden, my sister, my spouse: I have gathered my myrrh with my spices; I have eaten my bread with my honey; I have drunk my wine with my milk. Eat, O friends, and drink; yea, brethren, drink abundantly.

Song 4: 16- 5:1

Not only has she become nourishment to others around her, but now she has also become nourishment for her kinsman. She no longer has to wonder or ponder the presence of her beloved, because a unity has been forged between the maiden and her kinsman: a unity only the cross can accomplish. Confidence has replaced questioning and hesitation. Faith replaces doubting. Most of all, her spirit has become one with the Holy Spirit of God. There is also a constant and equal presence between the maiden's spirit and God's very own Holy Spirit. The illustration of the vine and branches in the Gospel of John 15:1-5 has become a reality with the maiden. That relationship between the vine and branches is one and the same between the maiden and the kinsman.

Not until we die (unto ourselves) can we live.

Until the mountain of myrrh and the hill of frankincense, the maiden, as much as she desired, couldn't return the kinsman's love. Now, dead, yet alive; she, by the union of their spirits, is able to fully return love to the kinsman. Before the cross, the maiden could only anticipate loving her kinsman. She couldn't truly love God: no not really. Oh, she wanted to love him. Yes, how she desired to love God, but the reality of love was only yet a dream. Now that she is truly alive, can she return love to her Lord? Now, and only now can she truly call God, "Abba, Father" (Romans 8:15).

Thanks be to God, he refuses to let us possess him as we so often attempt to do; or else we would never have the opportunity to experience the Lord's new wine: "All men at the beginning set forth good wine, then that which is worse. Not so with The Lord, "he hath kept back the good wine until now" (John 2:10 Tyndale): and this new wine can only be found on the other side of the mountain of myrrh and the hill of frankincense.

Moses gave (God thru Moses) the old nation Israel manna, but that was only until they were ready for what lay ahead: a land flowing with milk and honey, and how easily we too settle for manna when there is more, much more. Also, as the old nation Israel had to, by faith, cross the Jordon River before they could taste of the milk and honey of the Promised Land; we as the new nation Israel (Matthew 21:43),* to experience the new wine of the Lord, must go by faith to the mountain of myrrh and the hill of frankincense.

As good as things are with the maiden, there is more for her. Her spirit is now in union with the Holy Spirit, but that too is only a beginning. The kinsman will now bring the maiden's soul into union with her God, so the two are as one, but not until one more trial is set before her.

I sleep, but my heart is awake: the voice of my kinsman knocks at the door,
saying, open, open to me, my companion, my sister, my dove, my perfect
one: for my head is filled with dew, and my locks with the drops of the night.
Song 5:2

The maiden now lives almost exclusively in the spiritual realm. The physical world no longer holds any promise to her. Yes, she feeds, clothes, and rests her physical body, but she lives in the spirit.

Night comes, and the maiden's body sleeps, but her spirit remains awake all through the nights. The maiden no longer prays only while she is awake. She now prays night and day; asleep or awake, she prays. It matters not what her physical body does. She cares not for the things of this world. Also, as the maiden is in constant prayer, her kinsman works night and day as well.

I have put off my coat; how shall I put it on? I have washed my feet, how
shall I defile them? My kinsman put forth his hand by the hole of the
door, and my belly was moved for him. I rose up to open to my kinsman;
my hands dropped myrrh, my fingers choice myrrh, on the handles of
the lock.
Song 5:3-5

While the maiden is in prayer; even while sleeping: her kinsman knocks at her door. The first time the maiden was in bed (Song 3:1), we notice there, although tired, she couldn't sleep; in that she longed for her beloved. In fact, she arouse out of bed to search for her kinsman. Whereas, this time she is asleep yet awake in prayer, and this time the kinsman comes in search of her; not the other way around (Please note, The Lord is always working. Never is there a time he isn't working for the coming of the kingdom of God on earth as it is in heaven). However, this time, the maiden's reaction is very strange indeed. When her kinsman, whom she always longs for, knocks for her to open to him: She hesitates. She halters between two choices.

I have put off my coat; how shall I put it on?
Song 5:3

She wants to get up and open to her kinsman, yet, to do so would require her to put her coat on. Next, her feet were clean, and to get up to open to her kinsman would require her to get her feet dirty.

I have washed my feet, how shall I defile them?
Song 5:3

Does she open the door? It was cold, it was dirty. She was torn inside out.

...my belly was moved for him.
Song 5:4

Nevertheless, after some hesitation, she "rose up" to open to her kinsman. Then it happened. When her hand met his hand, she drew back. She had felt his wet myrrh soaked hand, and she recoiled. Immediately, he was gone. She had rejected him. She was offended by the touch of his hands. She ran after him wanting to make things right, but it was too late. She had rejected him. However slight, she had rejected him nevertheless.

What happened? Why was she offended by him?

The maiden had become comfortable in her new life with God. She had finally "arrived", and she became smug. She, for a moment, had forgotten where she had come from; consequently, she was offended by her Lord. She was warm and didn't want to go out in the cold. She was clean, and didn't want to get dirty again, and he was both wet and dirty from the work of the kingdom.

Yes, the work of the Lord is indeed offensive; and even those closest to him become offended, however the work must still be done. Who will join him? Who will defile their head with "the drops of the night"?

The maiden realized her mistake, but it was too late. Nevertheless, she ran after him hoping that there was some way to make up to him.

> *I opened to my kinsman; my kinsman was gone: my soul failed at his speech: I sought him, but found him not; I called him, but he answered me not. The watchman that go their rounds in the city found me, they smote me, they wounded me; the keepers of the walls took away my veil from me.*
>
> *Song 5:6, 7*

This time we notice that the watchman smote the maiden. Before (Song 3:3), they didn't give her much attention, however, now she was vastly different from them. They could tell she was favored among others. They could tell she had a special relationship to the kinsman. In short, they were jealous of the maiden: So, they came against her; and isn't it so typical her most trouble came from pastors, ministers, and priests. These from within always do more damage than those on the outside world. However, none of this mattered to the maiden. She knows she is his; and he is hers'; and her love for him is as strong as ever. She is still "wounded with love".

> *I have charged you, O daughters of Jerusalem, by the powers and the virtues of the field: if ye find my kinsman, what are ye to say to him? That I am wounded with love.*
>
> *Song 5:8*

The first time she used the phrase, "wounded with love" (Song 2:5), it was her way of expressing how the love of God feels. God's love is overwhelming, almost incapacitating, especially experiencing it for the first time. This time, however, being "wounded with love" comes from the fact the maiden is so deeply in love with her beloved that these feelings of love actually cut into the very core of her being; so much so, she is all but unable to function.

To have the love of God, then to have him disappear out of her life is almost too much to bear. Her spiritual life vanishes too. At least before when he left her he would eventually answer her, but this time there is nothing: "I sought him, but found him not;" (Song 5:6). Even praying, including praying the scriptures alludes her: "I called him, but he answered me not"

(Song 5:6). So she cries out to anyone that will hear her, thus a call to "O daughters of Jerusalem". They replied:

> *What is thy kinsman more than another kinsman, O thou beautiful among*
> *women? What is thy kinsman more than another kinsman, that thou hast*
> *so charged us?*
>
> *Song 5:9*

She asks for help in order to find her beloved, but these well meaning Christians can't understand what has the maiden so upset. They wonder if the maiden is over reacting a bit, but never having experienced the very love of God in their lives, as found at the 'mountain of myrrh and the hill of frankincense", they can't understand what it is to be "wounded with love" (That is, outside of that first kiss). As hard as they might want to understand, they simply cannot.

To understand the love of God we must accept God at his every word, but most church people say they will accept God when they can understand God. Sorry, but acceptance must and always comes before understanding. The maiden totally and fully abandoned all for the kinsman, consequently, she understands him. Just listen to her beautiful and complete description of the Lord and Savior.

> *My kinsman is white and ruddy, chosen out from myriads. His head is*
> *as very fine gold, his locks are flowing, black as a raven. His eyes are*
> *as doves, by the pools of waters, washed with milk, sitting by the pools.*
> *His cheeks are as bowls of spices pouring forth perfumes: his lips are*
> *lilies, dropping choice myrrh. His hands are as turned gold set with*
> *beryl: his belly is an ivory tablet on a sapphire stone. His legs are*
> *marble pillars set on golden sockets: his form is as Libanus, choice as*
> *the cedars. His throat is most sweet, and altogether desirable. This is*
> *my kinsman, and this is my companion, O daughters of Jerusalem.*
>
> *Song 5:10-16*

The maiden knows her kinsman; her Lord; her God. She knows him so much so that she can describe every characteristic of him, from the top of his head to the soles of his feet.

We are coming to see that a gulf exists between this maiden and all the others in church. The more she surrenders to her beloved the wider the gulf gets.

This is the last thing the maiden would want. She doesn't want to be different from the others, but love compels her; all the while others continue, "Sitting in the markets" (Matthew 11:16).

God doesn't want this either. He would that all were as the maiden ("Whosoever"; John 3:16). However, the choice is ours. For, he "piped unto you, and ye have not danced; he mourned unto you, and ye have not lamented" (Matthew 11:17). One way or the other, we each prove our salvation is or is not.

Oh, dear Christian, why do we find it so strange to be able to know God as the maiden knows him? However, let us not stop here. There is more. His wine keeps getting better and better.

To know him is to love him; and the maiden knows the kinsman, thus she loves him; and this despite the fact he had left her. Despite this, she knows right where the kinsman has gone, and right now, in his absence, she knows nothing can or ever will separate her from him; never, ever.

> *Whither is thy kinsman gone, thou beautiful among women?*
> *Whither has thy kinsman turned aside? Tell us, and we will*
> *seek him with thee. My kinsman is gone down to his garden,*
> *to beds of spice, to feed his flock in the gardens, and to gather*
> *lilies. I am my kinsman's and my kinsman is mine, who feeds*
> *among the lilies.*
>
> *Song 5:17- 6:2*

Not only does she know him; she also knows his comings and goings, and this while he is still absent from her: But others cannot seek him with her. Each person must seek him alone.

Don't get me wrong: There is no lone-ranger Christians. We all must live in fellowship with other Christians (Those that have truly been kissed "with the kisses of his mouth"). We are the church, and the church is one body with many members, all of which work together in unity to the fulfillment of the kingdom of heaven. God works all things thru the church and without the church God does nothing. Nevertheless, we here are in this Song dealing with each Christian's inward spiritual walk. This walk is a one on one journey, and no one can join with you. Here in the inward journey every Christian is alone.

Her kinsman now returns, and although, being wounded with love, and her prayer life all but non-existent, she still maintained her faith in God: As did Abraham: She, "against hope, still believed in hope" (Romans 4:18): and her kinsman acknowledges this great faith of hers.

> *Thou art fair, my companion, as pleasure, beautiful as Jerusalem,*
> *terrible as armies set in array. Turn away thine eyes from before*
> *me, for they have ravished me: Thy hair is as flocks of goats which*
> *have appeared from Galaad. Thy teeth are as flocks of shorn sheep,*
> *that have gone up from the washing, all of them bearing twins, and*
> *there is none barren among them: thy lips are as thread of scarlet,*
> *and thy speech is comely. Thy cheek is like the rind of a pomegranate,*
> *being seen without thy veil.*
>
> *Song 6:3-6*

No matter what failures the maiden has made, she still looks just as beautiful to her kinsman as ever. Even though the maiden was offended by the kinsman, she is still special to her Lord. She is still at the center of his affections. Try as she may, the maiden can never be less to her Lord.

Here we are reminded of Abraham, Moses, David and others where God had a special relationship with the saints of old. These great saints, at times, let God down too. However, despite punishment God still held these up as examples for others to follow. The maiden falls into this category. Yes, she may have let her beloved down at times, yet that will never change their relationship. In fact, the Lord said of our maiden and all those that have taken the journey of love:

Verily I say unto you, Among them that are born of woman there

hath not risen a greater than John the Baptist: notwithstanding he that
is least in the kingdom of heaven is greater than he.

Matthew 11:11 (KJV)

The time lapse between the maiden being offended by the kinsman and his return lasts into years for most. Regardless, everyone who travels this journey goes through this time of spiritual drought where faith and faith alone sustains the traveler.

* This is not replacement theology. You could call it relay theology. The old nation Israel carried the torch of witness for two thousand years (from Abraham to Christ). The church carries this torch for another two thousand years (Christ to present). Soon and very soon, at the second coming of Christ, the church will pass the torch back to the first nation Israel.

CHAPTER SEVEN

LIVING AMONG THE ANGELS

There are sixty queens, and eighty concubines, and maidens
without number. My dove, my perfect one is one; she is the
only one of her mother; she is the choice of her that bore her.
The daughters saw her, and the queens will pronounce her
blessed, yea, and the concubines, and they will praise her.
Who is this that looks forth as the morning fair as the moon,
choice as the sun, terrible as armies set in array?
Song 6:7-9

Not only has her beloved returned, but her spiritual and prayer life has exploded; so much so she is found living among the angels. She had nothing to do about this transformation. God did it to her, or better yet, obedience had done its' work in her life. She didn't up one day and decide to live among the angels. Nevertheless, there she was, in her spirit, in heaven, before all these angelic beings. More than that, however, she is found to be favored even among the angels themselves.

The Lord's love is as vast as the stars in the heavens. We know so little of God and the kingdom of heaven, but for those that obey the kinsman, despite their failings, are invited to enter into that kingdom and live among the angels.

When God asks us to suffer with him; it isn't to see if we can endure the pain, or to become some sort of super Christian. No, the suffering and sorrows saints carry is their right of passage to live among the, "sixty queens, and eighty concubines, and maidens without number". Yet, this privilege is not reserved only for the next life. To the contrary, the Holy Spirit is constantly preparing those who will experience now, in this life, the kingdom of heaven within their lives. However, this experience is not for the faint hearted; for, "from the days of John the Baptist until now the kingdom of heaven suffereth violence, and the violent take it by force" (Matthew 11:12). Yes, this journey of love is not for everyone, but is only for those To Whom It May Concern. Also, most, if not all of these living among the angels, are obscure, unbecoming nobodies in the church. In fact, many are not even members of any organized church. For, God is indeed jealous over his elect. So much so, he hides these chosen few as he hid Elijah (1Kings 17). "He that hath ears to hear, let him hear" (Matthew 11:15).

Although, these few are unknown to others in this physical realm, they, as the maiden, are singled out and exalted in the heavenlies. Many may not know these chosen few, but the angels are vividly aware of who they are. As God waited upon Job's prayers (Job 42:8), so too does the heavenly Father anxiously await the prayers of these hidden few. For, the prayers of this remnant are as close to God as the angels in heaven are to him: and, it is the prayers of this elect which will usher in the kingdom. At the same time, Satan sees these few as, "terrible as armies set in array", because the prayers of these that live among the angels are indeed as powerful as mighty advancing armies: for, only those that suffer with him can reign with him (2 Timothy 2:12).

*I went down to the garden of nuts, to look at the fruits of the valley,
to see if the vine flowered, if the pomegranates blossomed. There
I will give thee my breasts: My soul knew it not: it made me as the
chariots of Aminadab.*

Song 6:10, 11

While her spirit and prayers prevail among the angels, our maiden goes to her kinsman's garden to check the progress of the Lord's endeavors. The maiden has become an active and intricate part of the very work of the kinsman. His ways are her ways.

*Return, return, O Sunamite; return, return, and we will look at thee.
What will ye see in the Sunamite? She comes as bands of armies.*

Song 6:12

It isn't long before even heaven itself cannot contain the prayers of the maiden. Her prayers reverberate from heaven and are felt back in this world. Not only are her prayers like "armies set in array", in the spiritual realm; but those same prayers, likewise, move before her in the physical realm "as bands of armies". The maiden has become a force to be reckoned with in heaven and on earth: and with each prayer, the two worlds come closer and closer together, fulfilling, "Thy kingdom come. Thy will be done in earth, as it is in heaven" (Matthew 6:10).

Yes, dear Christian, Matthew chapter eleven has come alive in the maiden: "the kingdom of heaven suffereth violence, and the violent take it by force" (Matthew 11:12).

Can we now see who the violent are? Yes, they are those that obey the Shepard in embracing sorrow and suffering, and they abandon themselves to God, "with all thy heart, and with all thy soul, and with all thy mind" (Matthew 22:37). Anything less, "is like unto children sitting in the markets, and calling unto their fellows, and saying, We have piped unto you, and ye have not danced; we have mourned unto you, and ye have not lamented" (Matthew 11:16, 17).

"He that hath ears to hear, let him hear" (Matthew 11:15).

CHAPTER EIGHT

TOTAL SURRENDER

Thy steps are beautiful in shoes, O daughter of the prince: the
joints of thy thighs are like chains, the work of the craftsman.
Thy navel is as a turned bowl, not wanting liquor; thy belly is as
a heap of wheat set about with lilies. Thy two breasts are as two
fawns. Thy neck is as an ivory tower; thin eyes are as pools in
Esebon, by the gates of the daughter of many: thy nose is as the
tower of Libanus, looking toward Damascus. Thy head upon
thee is as carmel, and the curls of thy hair like scarlet; the king
is bound in the galleries. How beautiful art thou, and how sweet
art thou my love! This is thy greatness in thy delights: thou wast
made like a palm tree, and thy breasts to clusters. I said, I will
go up to the tree, I will take hold of its high boughs: and now shall
thy breasts be as clusters of the wine, and the smell of thy nose as
apples; and thy throat as good wine, going well with my kinsman,
suiting my lips and teeth.

Song 7:1-9

Each time the kinsman describes the maiden (4:1-5; 4:9-15; 6:3-6; and here), she becomes more and more full; more and more mature. Each step in her journey of love she becomes more and more the person God had intended her to be. Not only has she matured, she has become a mighty tower of strength.

I am my kinsman's, and his desire is toward me.
Song 7:10

Confidence abounds. She no longer needs, or even wants to possess her kinsman. She is secure in his love for her. She knows for sure the two are one. Their souls as well as their spirits are in complete unity and oneness. Not only does her Lord know her every thought and desire, but she now knows his every thought and desire for her. Truly her mind is the very mind of Christ (1Corinthians 2:16; Philippians 2:5).

Come, my kinsman, let us go forth into the field; let us lodge in the
villages; let us see if the vine has flowered, if the blossoms have
appeared, if the pomegranates have blossomed; there will I give thee
my breasts. The mandrakes have given a smell, and at our doors are
all kinds of choice fruits, new and old. O my kinsman, I have kept
them for thee.

Song 7:11-13

Total surrender! She holds nothing back from her beloved. Every thought; every care; every concern is his. In return, not only does she have the mind of Christ, she knows his every coming and going. She has become his companion, not just in ministry, but she is his companion in prayer. She prays for his needs.

Imagine being able to pray for God's needs. What an honor; what a privilege; what an awesome position; to have God wait for our prayers. Nevertheless, that is exactly what she is doing, and she is able to pray for God, because she is, likewise, able to pray the scriptures. In fact, she is in constant and continual prayer, even as she sleeps. *

The relationship between the kinsman and the maiden is a complete give and take relationship. He, from the beginning, has kept his eyes fastened on the maiden's every move and heartbeat. Now, her lone concern is to watch his every move and heartbeat, and in the process she is coming to know more and more his every thought and desire.

Imagine being completely and fully consumed by one's passion for God. Only full and complete surrender survives between God and the maiden, for she has truly surrendered all: "I give thee my breasts". Never again does she keep anything, nor any part of herself from him. He has become her all in all.

But, I've never seen anyone like this.

And you probably won't. Just as no one recognized that John the Baptist was Elijah: "And if ye will receive it, this is Elijah, which was for to come" (Matthew 11:14).

---

* Remember, she had lost the ability to pray the scriptures back in chapter four (Song 3:6-8). Nevertheless, after her last trial, praying the scriptures returned. We must always keep in mind it is the Holy Spirit that gives us this gift. We cannot just up and decide to pray the scriptures. It is a gift, and as quickly as this gift is given, it can be taken away again. Now please don't confuse praying the scriptures with the gifts of ministry as described in Romans 12; 1Corinthians 12; and Ephesians 4. Those gifts once given are never taken back. Praying the scriptures is like praying itself: There is an ebb and flow to prayer, and this movement of prayer is completely in the control of the precious Holy Spirit. We cannot will ourselves into praying. If we do, then, my friend, that isn't prayer. That is soul power at work. In fact, much too much of our praying is exactly that: Our own raw soul power at it's best; or worst, depending on your perspective. If prayer isn't from above, then it is best not to even pray. At these times it is best to simply come before the Lord and wait on him. If that takes days, weeks or even years, so be it. Prayer isn't an exercise; where the more you pray the better it becomes. That is rubbish. Prayer is a lifestyle; a lifestyle and inward journey. More specifically, it is a relationship to a person; the person of the beloved Abba, Father. Nor is prayer a principle that adheres to certain basic truths with a set of functions, or a standard set of guidelines to ascribe to. That, my fellow Christian, is mind games, and reduces prayer to being nothing but a technique to be developed. Prayer does not come from the mind: it comes from the heart, and strikes at the very heart of the Father in heaven.

Praying the scriptures is praying during the reading of God's Word. It is a harmony of scriptures and prayer, both having come from above and found at our center where our spirit meets the Holy Spirit. In praying the scriptures, we can know what the Father's cares and concerns are. After all, the Bible was given by him, and all we are doing is giving back to him what he first gave us. More than that, in the process, we are given the opportunity to participate with Him in the daily functioning of, "Thy kingdom come…in earth, as it is in heaven" (Matthew 6:10).

CHAPTER NINE

AS A SEAL UPON THY HEART

I would that thou, O my kinsman, wert he that sucked the breasts of my mother; when I found thee without, I would kiss thee; yea, they should not despise me. I would take thee, I would bring thee into my mother's house, and into the chamber of her that conceived me; I would make thee to drink of spiced wine, of the juice of my pomegranates.

Song 8:1, 2

She is totally in love with her Lord. She says she loves the beloved with all her heart, and with all her soul, and with all her mind. There is nothing left to give him. She has given it all. He completely occupies her every thought, and there is no room left in her life for anything else. Again, he is her all in all.

From the beginning, God, through Moses, has said, "you shalt find him if thou seek him with all thy heart and with all thy soul" (Deuteronomy 4:29). The maiden has done this.

His left hand should be under my head, and his right hand should embrace me. I have charged you, ye daughters of Jerusalem, by the virtues of the field, that ye stir not up, nor awake my love, until he please.

Song 8:3, 4

For the third time (2:6; 3:5; and here) the shepherd gives instructions to all spiritual beings that this maiden is his, and hands off. He is jealous over his chosen. No one is even to make a sound so much as to awaken her while she sleeps.

Even now, the maiden needs time to just rest and gather strength. She still has a physical body, and even she succumbs to fatigue. Thus, in her times of weakness or rest her kinsman is forever protecting her.

Who is this that comes up all white, leaning on her kinsman? I raised thee up under an apple-tree; there thy mother brought thee forth; there she that bore thee brought thee forth.

Song 8:5

Finally, she can be with him, and not try and take possession of him. He can now stay with her without the maiden seeking to control or hold on to him. He no longer needs to come and go, for she has learned how to simply lean on his everlasting arm without grabbing or holding on to him. He is hers' and she is his, and she need not prove it; it just is.

Her every desire is fulfilled. The two are one, yet each is complete in themselves. They are as one, yet there are two of them. He that has always been is one with she that was, "chosen in him, before the foundation of the world was laid, that we should be saints, and without blame before him, through love" (Ephesians 1:4 Tyndale).

Also, this verse in <u>The Song</u> vividly portrays the fulfillment of: "Come unto me, all ye that labor and are heavy laden, and I will give you rest. Take my yoke upon you, and learn of me; for I am meek and lowly in heart: and ye shall find rest unto your souls. For my yoke is easy, and my burden is light" (Matthew 11:28-30). Our maiden has indeed found rest for her soul.

> *Set me as a seal upon thy heart, as a seal upon thine arm; for love is*
> *strong as death; jealousy is cruel as the grave, her shafts are shafts*
> *of fire, even the flames thereof. Much water will not be able to quench*
> *love, and rivers shall not drown it; if a man would give all his substance*
> *for love, men would utterly despise it.*
>
> *Song 8:6, 7*

The relationship is sealed with the Holy Spirit of God, "as a seal upon thy heart". Nothing, and I mean nothing, can undo what has been done between she and her God. Not even death can separate the maiden from her Lord, for love overcomes even death. Fire, water, the grave; none of these can overcome love. Even wealth cannot overcome love. In fact, wealth despises love.

There is one way and one way only to obtain this love; and that is through the walk of faith. God's love is a journey: a journey of love that God sets before us in order for each to be able to come into complete unity with Him. Then and only then can we, "love the Lord thy God with all thy heart, and with all thy soul, and with all thy mind. This is the first and great commandment" (Matthew 22:37, 38).

> *Our sister is little, and has no breasts; what shall we do for our sister,*
> *in the day wherein she shall be spoken for? If she is a wall, let us*
> *build upon her silver bulwarks; and if she is a door, let us carve for*
> *her cedar panels. I am a wall, and my breasts are as towers; I was in*
> *their eyes as one that found peace. Solomon had a vineyard in Beelamon;*
> *he let his vineyard to keepers; every one was to bring for its fruit a*
> *thousand pieces of silver. My vineyard, even mine, is before me.*
> *Solomon shall have a thousand, and they that keep its fruit two hundred.*
> *Thou that dwellest in the gardens, the companions hearken to thy voice:*
> *make me hear it.*
>
> *Song 8:8-13*

The moment the maiden obtained her goal of being one with her kinsman, is the moment she sent him away. She sent her beloved kinsman to her sister. Her sister is as she was before God, "kissed her with the kisses of his mouth" (Song 1:2).

Yes, the moment we come to, "love the Lord thy God with all thy heart, and with all thy soul, and with all thy mind", is the moment we come to "love thy neighbor as thyself. On these two commandments hang all the law and the prophets" (Matthew 22:37, 39, 40).

> *Away, my kinsman, and be like a doe or a fawn on the mountain of spices.*
> *Song 8:14*

35

Those that love God will take that love to others. She finally had her kinsman all to herself and her first action with him alone is to send him away. That loves as God loves. Her journey is complete. She now loves with the love of God. In fact, she is consumed by her love for God until she can say along with her beloved: "My meat is to do the will of him that sent me, and to finish his work. Say not ye, there are yet four months, and then come harvest? Behold, I say unto you, lift up your eyes, and look on the fields; for they are white already to harvest…both he that soweth and he that reapeth may rejoice together" (John 4:34-36).

Now abideth faith, hope, love, these three;
but the greatest of these is love.

1Corinthians 13:13